WALKERTON ELEMENTARY
SCHOOL LIBRARY

SUBMARINES

Modern Military Techniques

MODERN MILITARY TECHNIQUES
SUBMARINES

Tony Gibbons

Illustrations by
Tony Gibbons • Peter Sarson • Tony Bryan

Lerner Publications Company • Minneapolis

This book is available in two editions:
Library binding by Lerner Publications Company
Soft cover by First Avenue Editions
241 First Avenue North
Minneapolis, Minnesota 55401

This edition copyright © 1987 by Lerner Publications Company.
Original edition copyright © 1985 by Nomad Publishers Ltd.,
London, England.

All rights to this edition reserved by Lerner Publications Company.
No part of this book may be reproduced, stored in a retrieval system,
or transmitted in any form or by any means, electronic, mechanical,
photocopying, recording, or otherwise, without the prior written
permission of the Publisher except for the inclusion of brief quotations
in an acknowledged review.

Library of Congress Cataloging-in-Publication Data

Gibbons, Tony.
  Submarines.

  (Modern military techniques)
  Includes index.
  Summary: Examines the functions and design features of modern
submarines, both conventional diesel-powered and nuclear, and
focuses on such warfare aspects as tactics, missiles, and torpedoes.
  1. Submarine boats—Juvenile literature. 2. Submarine warfare—
Juvenile literature. 3. Anti-submarine warfare—Juvenile literature.
[1. Submarines. 2 Submarine warfare] I. Sarson, Peter, ill. II. Bryan,
Tony, ill. III. Title. IV. Series.
V857.G47   1987   623.8′257   86-10702
ISBN 0-8225-1383-8 (lib. bdg.)
ISBN 0-8225-9542-7 (pbk.)

Manufactured in the United States of America

    5   6   7   8   9   10   95   94   93   92   91   90

CONTENTS

1
First Generation of the Modern Submarine

All the modern submarines are directly descended from the German Type XXI, introduced towards the end of the Second World War. Its closed-cycle turbine engine enabled it to recycle its oxygen and so "breathe" underwater and maneuver and attack at high speed while entirely submerged. Its hull was more streamlined, offering less resistance to the water, with the conning tower, or "fin," enclosing two remotely-controlled gun turrets. A more commodious hull enabled more batteries to be carried to increase its underwater range.

Several of these submarines fell into Allied hands in 1945 and from the type the Russian *Whiskey* and *Zulu* classes were developed.

The USA also took the best features of the German vessel, and eventually abandoning the original highly unstable hydrogen-peroxide based fuel, they developed a safer diesel-electric submarine. In the early 1950s they introduced the "teardrop" shaped hull, a much more slender fin, and a single, slow-revving propeller. Hydroplanes, or wings, on the fin provided control in combination with a second, stern-mounted set of hydroplanes grouped near the rudder. This combination gave their test submarine *Albacore* a top speed of over 30 knots, a greater speed than any anti-submarine vessel likely to be deployed against it.

But the major step in submarine technology came in 1954 when the United States introduced *Nautilus,* the first nuclear-powered vessel. Now fully independent of the surface, it could cruise beneath the waves indefinitely, only limited by the endurance of its crew.

Below: Frantically completed towards the end of World War II, the German 2,100 ton *Type XXI* submarine was created in an attempt to offset the losses among the German U-boat forces. Its clean, streamlined hull had the underwater speed of 16 knots. It revolutionized submarine design.

Bottom: The *US Nautilus* of 1954, the first vehicle of any kind to be propelled by nuclear power

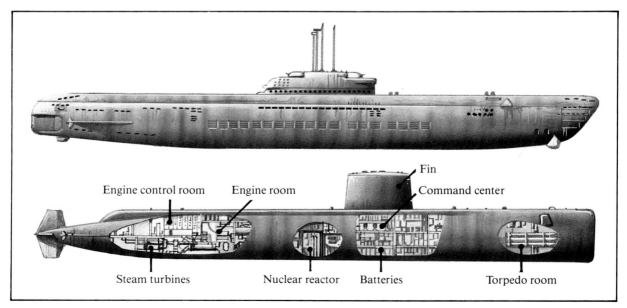

Engine control room   Engine room   Fin   Command center

Steam turbines   Nuclear reactor   Batteries   Torpedo room

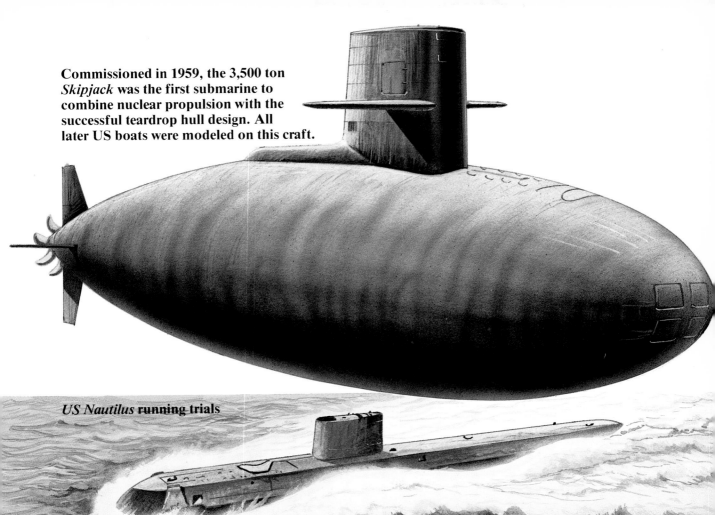

Commissioned in 1959, the 3,500 ton *Skipjack* was the first submarine to combine nuclear propulsion with the successful teardrop hull design. All later US boats were modeled on this craft.

US Nautilus **running trials**

Modern submarines

There are several different types of submarines, specialized for different purposes.

Conventional submarines (SS) The standard conventional submarine is the most common and features in the navies of most countries. These craft are used to patrol and defend friendly coastlines against attack and to prevent free use of the sea for the purposes of moving troops and supplies.

Attack submarines (SSN) Larger and more sophisticated than conventional submarines, these nuclear submarines have a great range and can operate away from friendly forces for long periods. They are used for hunting and tracking enemy shipping and destroying enemy nuclear-armed missile submarines.

Strategic missile submarines (SSBN) This is a completely new type of submarine, which is in effect a moving and hidden launch platform for nuclear missiles. Able to cruise underwater for vast distances armed with its deadly weapons, these submarines threaten retaliation should any country make first use of nuclear weapons, so acting as a threat to prevent an outbreak of war.

Cruise missile submarines (SSG) These submarines remain near friendly bases and carry small rocket-powered missiles that can be used against groups of surface ships or nearby land targets.

Rescue and research submarines While research submarines are equipped to explore the oceans and further the development of submarines generally, an important role carried out by some submarines is the rescue of survivors from another submarine or the retrieval of material from the floor of the ocean.

2 Modern Conventional Submarines (SS)

The conventional diesel-powered submarine appears comparatively unimportant when set against the imposing bulk of its larger nuclear-powered rivals, yet it occupies an important place in the inventories of many navies of today.

It is relatively low in cost compared to the larger and more sophisticated attack submarines, such as the US *Los Angeles*. It also needs fewer crew. When running submerged on electric motors it makes little noise and is not easily detected. This makes it ideal for patrol and reconnaissance duties.

Conventional submarines can be divided into three groups, based on their size. The small 400 to 600 ton coastal type is suitable for inshore shallow water. Although effective in many roles, it is hampered by poor range, few torpedo reloads and limited sensor equipment.

The 900 to 1300 ton type make up the second group. Examples are the German *Type 209*, the Swedish *Sjöormen* and the French *Daphne*. The latter even has microphones set around the hull so that those inside can monitor noise levels and control their craft accordingly. These submarines are all ideal for smaller navies with medium range tasks.

The final group comprises the largest conventional boats, which range from 1600 tons upwards. The Dutch *Walrus* class and the Royal Navy's *Oberon* class are examples, while the Russian *Tango* at 3700 tons is at the top of the range.

In spite of improvements, such as a more streamlined hull and stronger batteries, the type still suffers from limited underwater endurance and must spend time just beneath the surface running its engines in order to recharge batteries.

Perhaps the most advanced conventional type under construction is the Royal Navy's *Vickers Type 2400*, but it may prove too costly for likely overseas customers. The US Navy has not encouraged the development of conventional boats, preferring to rely on nuclear propulsion. Russia and her allies, however, still operate over 249 conventional submarines.

Smaller navies today are keen to increase their conventional submarine forces and in addition, many are now able to build these craft themselves.

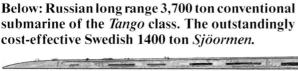

Below: Russian long range 3,700 ton conventional submarine of the *Tango* class. The outstandingly cost-effective Swedish 1400 ton *Sjöormen*.

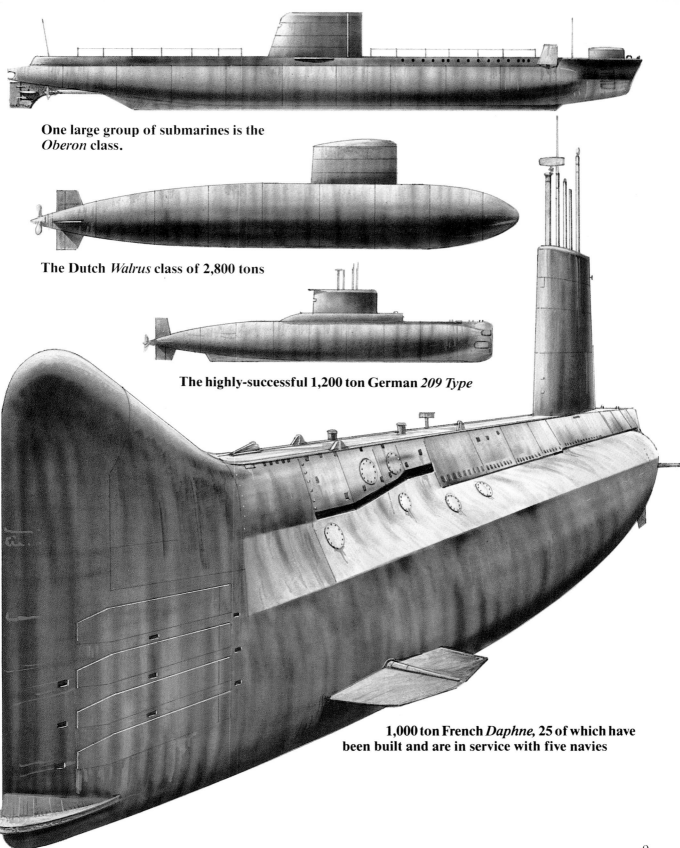

One large group of submarines is the *Oberon* class.

The Dutch *Walrus* class of 2,800 tons

The highly-successful 1,200 ton German *209 Type*

1,000 ton French *Daphne,* 25 of which have been built and are in service with five navies

3 Modern Attack Submarines (SSN)

The modern nuclear-powered attack submarine is designed for three main functions. As a hunter/killer it must use its sophisticated electronic sensing equipment to seek out and destroy opposing submarines. It is used as an independent forward attack and reconnaissance unit and as an escort to protect task groups and convoys against enemy submarines and surface vessels.

All this would take place in the silent depths of the ocean, where opponents do not see each other. Success depends on quietness. The *Los Angeles*, which displaces 50 percent more than earlier US attack submarines, is also much quieter. The large hull effectively deadens much of the noise of the engines. It has a maximum speed of about 34 knots. Many of these US boats are stationed in the Atlantic, ready to defend its sea lanes in the event of a European war.

The UK followed US developments in submarines for a time, but later classes are original British designs. The HMS *Resolution* is typical of the type, while the *Trafalgar* class is a recent development.

The first Russian nuclear boats were the *November* class, introduced in 1958 and produced as a result of intensive intelligence gathering rather than original research. They were said to have a surface speed of 20 knots, a submerged speed of 25 knots, but these boats were noisier than their US counterparts.

The *Victor* class introduced by the USSR in 1967-68 were much quieter and believed to be capable of 30 knots underwater. The number of attack submarines has recently been increased still

further by converting some missile boats, though these conversions may not have been as effective as purpose-built vessels.

In the 1970s, Russia started to bring in the *Alfa* class, credited with a speed of over 42 knots. These submarines are powered by a smaller nuclear reactor, so enabling the vessel to be reduced in size. They are built of titanium and the added strength of this material enables them to dive to depths of about 3,016 feet (914 m).

HMS Swiftsure, **1973**

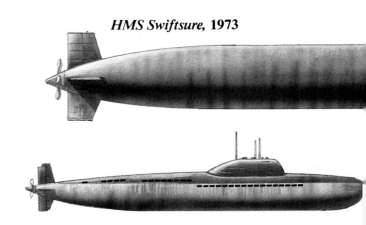

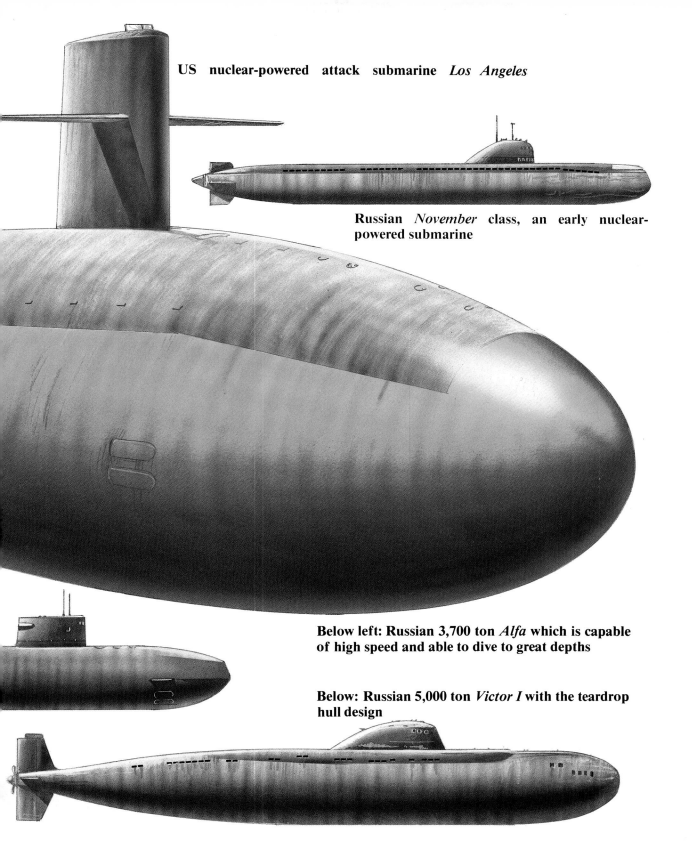

US nuclear-powered attack submarine *Los Angeles*

Russian *November* class, an early nuclear-powered submarine

Below left: Russian 3,700 ton *Alfa* which is capable of high speed and able to dive to great depths

Below: Russian 5,000 ton *Victor I* with the teardrop hull design

4 Missile Submarines (SSBN)

By 1955 both the Russian and American navies were engaged in a furious search for an effective submarine launched ballistic missile which could be fired from any point within the enormous scope of a nuclear submarine. Russia converted six *Zulu* class submarines to fire ballistic missiles and this prompted the United States to develop a similar system, eventually resulting in the Polaris missile.

The problems with the first Sea-Launched Ballistic Missiles (SLBM) were that they had to be launched dangerously close to the enemy's coastline and they had to be launched on the surface.

Polaris overcame these problems because it was a great deal smaller than previous missiles and was launched by cold gas. This enabled it to be fired from a submerged submarine. It had a range of 1,332.6 miles (2,221 km), yet it was so small that sixteen could be fitted in the hull of a submarine. This long range allowed the submarine to hide far out at sea and made the vessel virtually undetectable before it launched its weapons, while the Russian submarines had to come close to the American coastline and surface before firing.

The US Navy acquired five modified *George Washington* class nuclear ballistic missile submarines (SSBN) with Polaris by 1961. In the 1970s the improved Poseidon C3 missiles replaced Polaris.

Meanwhile, a new program was under development, to produce a much longer range missile. The Trident SLBM has a range of over 4,200 miles (7,000 km) and needed a new submarine designed to accommodate it. The *Ohio* class submarine now entering service is designed to take Trident missiles. It was the largest US submarine ever built, at 18,700 tons.

Russia developed several groups, culminating in the massive 13,250 ton *Delta III,* with its distinctive hump back housing 16 SSN-18 missiles.

The *Ohio* was considered vast until the advent of the monster 25,000 ton Russian *Typhoon* class, carrying 20 new type missiles in front of its fin. Because of the increased range of the modern missiles, the size of these boats is not such a disadvantage as they can be stationed near home in safe waters, well protected from enemy forces. This makes it very difficult to destroy the missiles before they are fired.

Britain and France have their own small independent nuclear forces of missile submarines, totaling fifteen units. However, only about one third of these are ever on station, so they would be at great risk if the Russians made a major breakthrough in anti-submarine warfare.

18,700 ton US *Ohio,* built to carry 24 Trident missiles

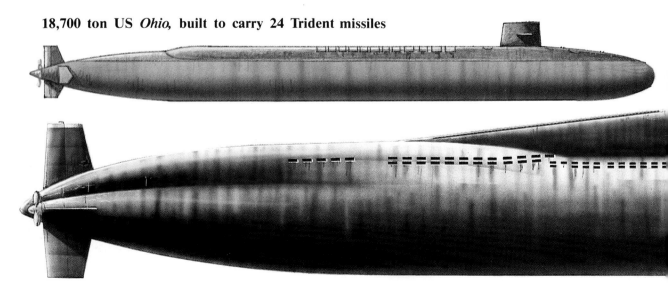

Above: Russian 25,000 ton *Typhoon* **launching one of its deadly missiles from the safety of the ocean depths**

Below: Russian nuclear-powered *Delta III* **of 13,250 tons armed with 16 giant SS-N-8 missiles**

5 Submarine Design Features

The two submarines shown here are both attack submarines, armed with torpedoes, yet they contrast greatly in their sophistication.

Top, is the Swedish *Sjöormen* patrol submarine, designed for operations in the Baltic. It is a middle-sized conventional submarine, limited to some degree by the dictates of cost. It can operate with only 17 crew, of whom at least 40 percent would be highly-trained officers, which shows the high technical content of its machinery. It can go to a depth of 495 feet (150 m), has a speed of 15 to 20 knots and can remain at sea for three weeks. High speed turbo charged diesels are situated under the main deck and a large volume of batteries carried amidships low down to aid stability.

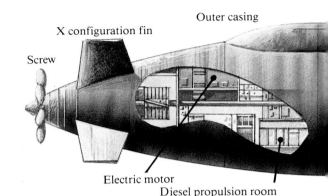

X configuration fin

Outer casing

Screw

Electric motor

Diesel propulsion room

The *Swiftsure*, in contrast, is nuclear powered and an extremely potent fighting machine. It can operate against other submarines and surface ships as a hunter/killer. This boat is 273.9 feet (83 m) long with a beam of 32.34 feet (9.8 m). Its displacement is 4,500 tons submerged and speed underwater is 30 knots. It has five torpedo tubes with 20 reloads and sub-harpoon anti-ship missiles.

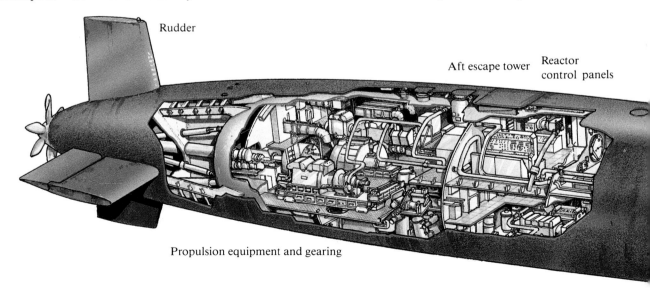

Rudder

Aft escape tower

Reactor control panels

Propulsion equipment and gearing

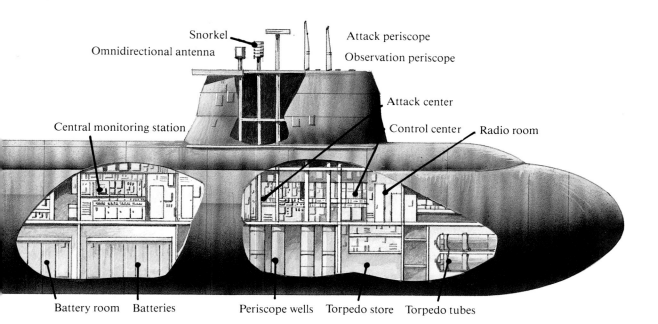

Snorkel

Omnidirectional antenna

Attack periscope

Observation periscope

Central monitoring station

Attack center

Control center   Radio room

Battery room   Batteries

Periscope wells   Torpedo store   Torpedo tubes

Reloading a torpedo tube can be accomplished in 15 seconds. Crew number twelve officers and 85 men. Initial building cost was about $52 million per submarine and they cost about $7 million a year to run.

Below: The 4,500 ton *Swiftsure* of the Royal Navy. These vessels carry Tigerfish torpedoes with a range of about 19.2 miles (32 km). Because of a cleaner hull design, the internal volume of the hull is greatly increased, giving more space for equipment and providing better living conditions

Radar mast

Attack periscope

Search periscope

Conning tower

Control room

Wardroom

Forward escape tower

Sonar

Crew deck

Torpedo stowage

Torpedo tubes

Hydroplane

Transducer fairings

6
Missile Submarine Design Features

The nuclear missile submarine represents the most potent naval weapon available, carrying an awesome destructive force. It is designed not as a fighting vessel, although it carries torpedoes, but rather as a gigantic mobile missile launching platform. The huge missiles, with ranges of thousands of miles, could each destroy a city.

The great range of the missiles and the fact that they are launched from underwater mean that these submarines can patrol in waters far removed from the enemy targets. They have the oceans of the world in which to hide and they can avoid contact with the outside world for long periods of time.

It is important that they remain hidden because

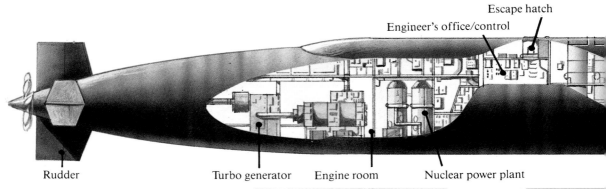

Rudder   Turbo generator   Engine room   Nuclear power plant

Escape hatch
Engineer's office/control

The giant nuclear-powered *Ohio* class showing various internal sections of the vessel. Note the amount of space devoted to the complex missile stowage and the numerous deck levels. These are among the most sophisticated weapons ever built and almost impossible to detect when hiding in the ocean. Inset shows a missile being launched from an *Ohio* class submarine from near the polar ice cap.

if one country was aiming to start a war with another, it would know that its enemy had armed submarines waiting to fire their missiles. It would not know where to find those submarines and so could not destroy them first. As the submarines would fire back if their home country was attacked there would be no point in starting a war with this huge threat hidden away at sea and this is the idea of nuclear deterrence.

The United States keeps about half its SSBNs on station, with the rest under refit or training. The SSBN usually reaches its assigned station at high speed, then proceeds to cruise at only about 2 or 3 knots. Russia, by comparison, retains a smaller number, about fifteen, on station.

In the *Ohio* class, a new more powerful reactor is used, which is also quieter than previous vessels because of its natural circulation design. Great attention has been paid to noise reduction and the expensive quietness techniques have made it more economical to carry more missiles per submarine rather than build more vessels.

The reactor is housed aft of the center of the vessel, feeding the engines in the aft section of the hull. Missile tubes are housed in the midship section, with the control area and crew quarters forward. Right in the nose is a large sonar sphere.

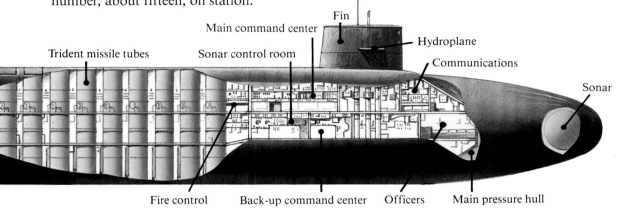

Trident missile tubes · Main command center · Sonar control room · Fin · Hydroplane · Communications · Sonar

Fire control · Back-up command center · Officers · Main pressure hull

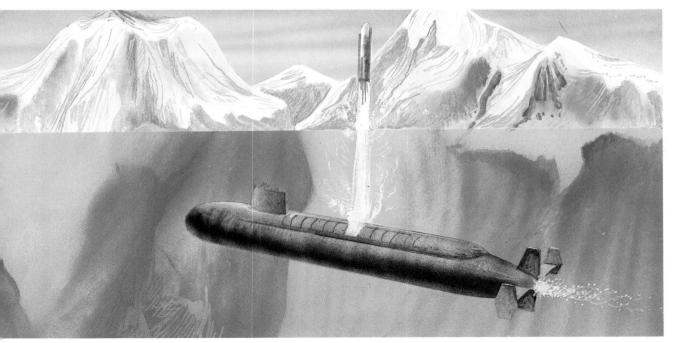

7
How the
Submarine
Works

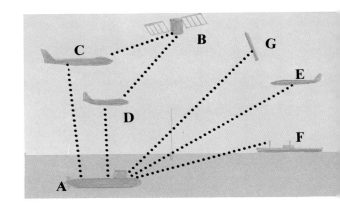

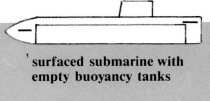

' surfaced submarine with
empty buoyancy tanks

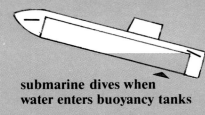

submarine dives when
water enters buoyancy tanks

with tanks filled to correct
level the submarine levels off

How a submarine dives

Early submarine hulls, because of their long slender proportions, tended to pitch up and down at relatively high speed, which led to poor horizontal control. With the introduction of the teardrop-shaped hull, the submarine became dynamically stable at speed and yet was easy to dive.

The new hull design, with its greater ratio of beam to length, made multi-deck boats possible and for a given floor space, smaller boats were possible.

These smaller boats, in turn, offered less resistance and with their streamlined hulls, they could travel faster for a given powerplant.

Ballast tanks, the spaces between the inner and outer hull, stretch from the stern of the missile room to the propeller and from the fin, forward to

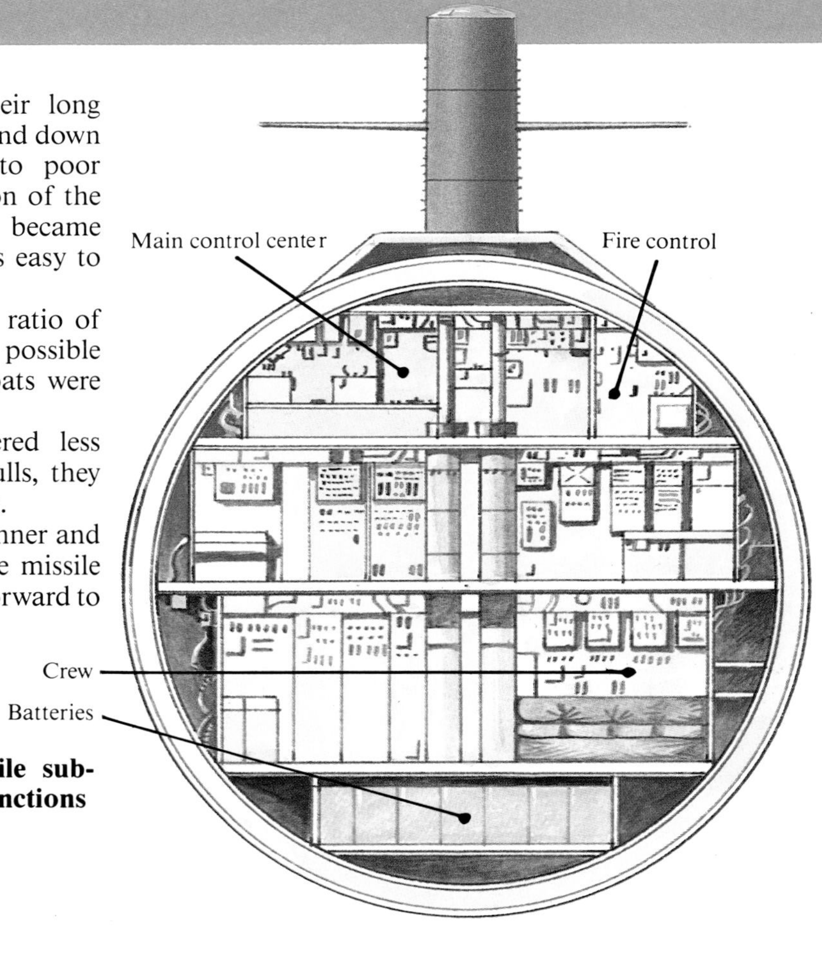

Main control center

Fire control

Crew

Batteries

View through a modern Trident missile submarine, showing the various levels and functions

18

The costly and complicated methods which are used to retain touch with a missile-armed submarine. A ballistic missile submarine, B satellite with overall view, C national emergency command, D local communications aircraft, E Long-range surveillance, F surface ships, G emergency rocket.

methods enable many modern submarines to reach depths of over 1,980 feet (600 m), where it is even more difficult to find them because of the different layers of water.

Conventional submarines have diesel engines, which need air in which to work. They are only used when the submarine is surfaced or at periscope depth, which is about 50 feet (15 m). A long tube is used, called a snorkel, which sucks down air from above the waves and so allows the engines to work. Below periscope depth the main motors are

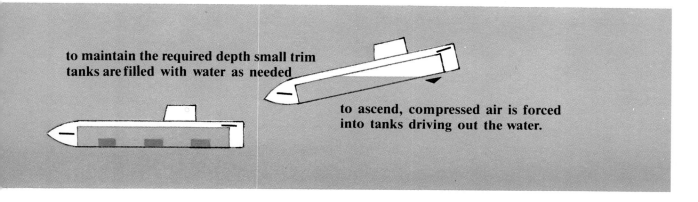

to maintain the required depth small trim tanks are filled with water as needed

to ascend, compressed air is forced into tanks driving out the water.

the bows. Once submerged, the submarine must have its weight distribution adjusted to remain level. This is done by transferring water to and from trim tanks within the main hull.

To dive, the ballast tanks are filled with sea water through valves in the bottom of the tanks so that the submarine sinks. To surface, the water is expelled from the ballast tanks by releasing air pressure through the main vents in the tanks' tops. As the submarine becomes more buoyant, it rises. The hydroplanes are used to control the angle of the ascent or descent.

As a submarine goes deeper, so the compression of the hull increases and the displacement becomes less. By expelling water from the trim tanks, the displacement can be adjusted so that it equals its weight and the submarine is able to hover without any aid from its engines or hydroplanes.

The strength of the pressure hull determines the depth to which a submarine can dive. The hull is pierced by as few apertures as possible, and improvements in materials and construction

supplied with power by the many large batteries carried. These are recharged by the diesel engines when the submarine snorkels or regains the surface. Conventional diesel-powered submarines must surface or snorkel regularly to recharge batteries and to release poisonous exhaust fumes.

By contrast, the nuclear powered submarine is totally independent of the surface and can cruise beneath the waves indefinitely. This is made possible by the nuclear reactor which produces no exhaust and is fueled by a tiny amount of uranium. An average submarine could go around the world seven times without refueling.

The nuclear reactor acts like a boiler. Coolant liquid is pumped in a closed circuit between the reactor, where it absorbs heat from the radioactive core and a heat exchanger. The coolant gives off heat to water in a secondary system, which produces steam to drive the turbines.

Steam also powers a generator which produces electricity to run the subsidiary systems on the boat and to keep the batteries charged.

8
How the Submarine "Sees" and "Hears"

Originally, submarines had shallow conning towers inset with small portholes through which the commander caught glimpses of his victim. In 1903, the periscope was introduced which meant that the submarine was no longer blind once it dived beneath the surface. The periscope is a long thin tube which has several mirrors positioned inside it; these turn the image around the corner and carry it down to an eye piece set in a base.

There are two main requirements for an efficient periscope. A large lens is important because it will gather more light and create a better picture, and the length of the tube is also vital. There is a large periscope and a smaller one, difficult to detect from the air on most submarines.

Periscopes now have many refinements. Infra-

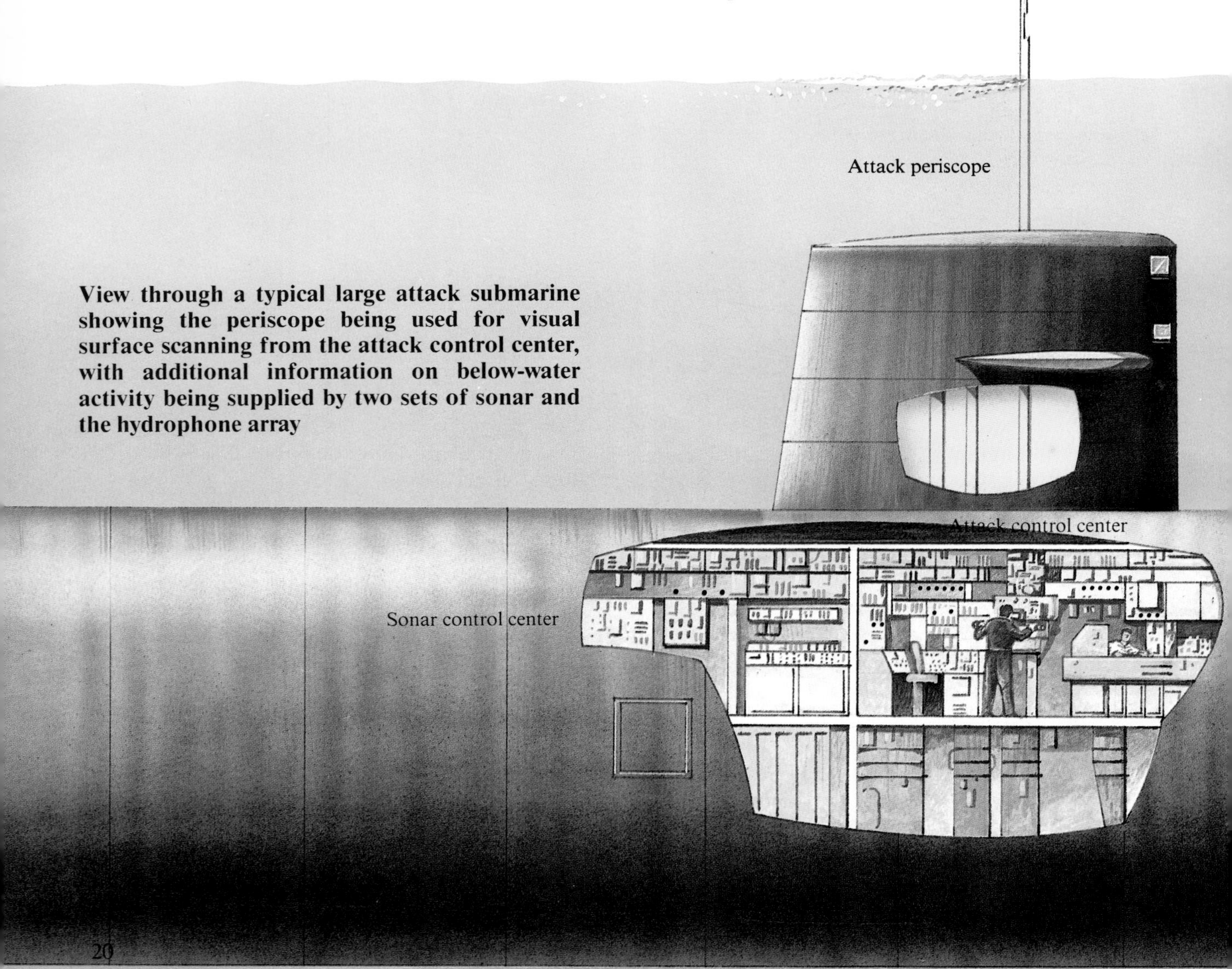

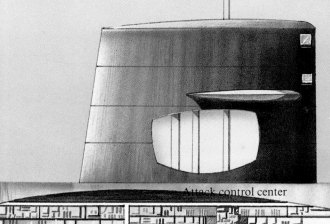

Attack periscope

View through a typical large attack submarine showing the periscope being used for visual surface scanning from the attack control center, with additional information on below-water activity being supplied by two sets of sonar and the hydrophone array

Attack control center

Sonar control center

red detection and image intensification are very useful for seeing at night without being seen oneself. Stabilization and automatic target tracking equipment also make the periscope more useful.

To "hear" what is going on around it while submerged, the submarine uses sonar. This stands for Sound Navigation Ranging. It is usually located in the nose of the submarine so as to be well clear of any interference from the noise of the submarine's own engines.

The sonar either listens to the noises around it (passive sonar) or emits a short inaudible pulse of sound which travels out at a given point (active sonar). If it strikes an object, the sound waves travel back and register on a screen. The time they take to return and the direction of the echoes indicate the position of the enemy. Active sonar has one disadvantage. Its noise may be picked up by enemy sonar. So many submarines just use passive sonar which simply picks up any sounds in the area.

When at sea, the usual practice of fixing a ship's position was by star sights and radio fixes. Neither of these is possible for a nuclear submarine and anyway, a higher standard of navigation is required. This was achieved with a system called Ships Inertial Navigation System (SINS) which is a complex set of gyroscopes that record every movement made by the submarine after it leaves a fixed position. The information is fed into the main computer to continually update the submarine's position in relation to its likely targets.

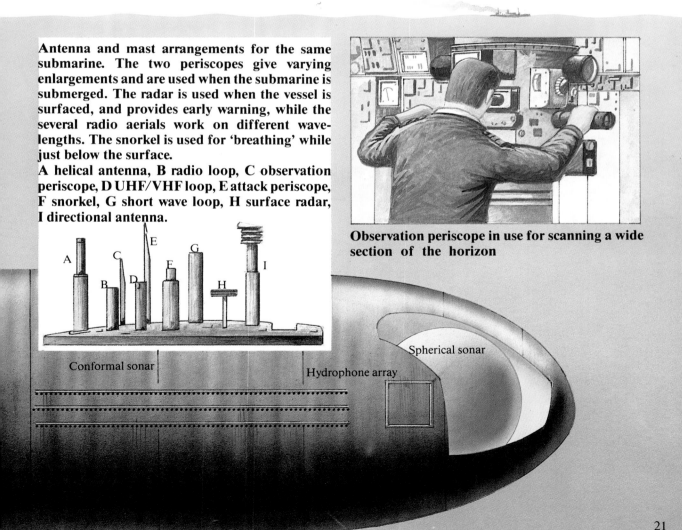

Antenna and mast arrangements for the same submarine. The two periscopes give varying enlargements and are used when the submarine is submerged. The radar is used when the vessel is surfaced, and provides early warning, while the several radio aerials work on different wavelengths. The snorkel is used for 'breathing' while just below the surface.
A helical antenna, B radio loop, C observation periscope, D UHF/VHF loop, E attack periscope, F snorkel, G short wave loop, H surface radar, I directional antenna.

A

C

E

B

D

E

G

H

I

Observation periscope in use for scanning a wide section of the horizon

Conformal sonar

Hydrophone array

Spherical sonar

9 Submarines at War: Methods of Attack

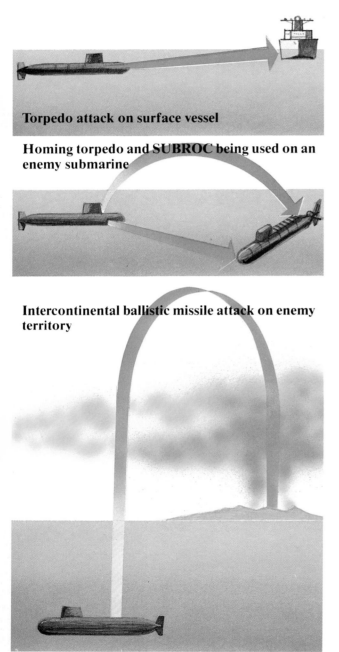

Torpedo attack on surface vessel

Homing torpedo and SUBROC being used on an enemy submarine

Intercontinental ballistic missile attack on enemy territory

Tactical Weapons

Unlike the submarines of the past which had as their main targets enemy ships, today's submarines have two main missions. The first is to wage war against enemy warships, submarines and merchant ships. This is known as tactical warfare.

One object is to impede the free use of sea lanes by the enemy by attacking his vessels at every opportunity. Conventional submarines can fulfil this role using their torpedoes. As well as weakening the enemy's navy, attack submarines might carry out operations against merchant vessels in order to deny them free passage on the ocean to carry supplies to armies or troops that might threaten friendly shores.

Another tactical use is the hunting down and destruction of enemy submarines. For this, the weapon used may be SUBROC, which is a missile launched from a torpedo tube. It has a range of about 33.6 miles (56 km). Cruise-type anti-ship and anti-submarine missiles are also carried by attack submarines. These are fired from the torpedo tubes, but their flight is powered by a jet engine and electronic guidance allows them to fly low enough over the sea to escape detection. These may also be used against military targets on the land. The Tomahawk, for example, has a range of 300 miles (500 km).

Strategic Missiles

However, another type of weapon altogether is carried by specially-built submarines. Strategic nuclear missiles are the most potent weapon available and they are designed for use against distant land targets. These Submarine Launched Ballistic Missiles (SLBMs) such as the Polaris and Trident have immense destructive power and ranges of thousands of miles. Their launch would mean the start of a nuclear war. Only the superpowers and some other large nations need to arm themselves with these strategic weapons.

German-designed *209 Type* conventional submarine preparing to carry out a torpedo attack against an enemy patrol craft

10 Tactical Weapons of the Submarine

The main armament of conventional and nuclear-powered hunter/killer submarines is the torpedo. Torpedoes come in several types. The basic battery-powered, free running torpedo travels at about 36 miles per hour (60 km/h). Conventional torpedo attack is carried out against a surface vessel by tracking at periscope depth, then firing several quick salvos. Torpedo tubes can be reloaded quite quickly by mechanical systems, though the number of torpedoes carried is severely limited by the space available.

A torpedo that came into service some time ago in the US Navy is the modified Mk 16, weighing 4,796 pounds (2,180 kg), 20.625 feet (6.25 m) long, with a diameter of 21.32 inches (533 mm). This model, propelled by hydrogen peroxide, carries a 880-pound (400-kg) warhead intended for use against surface ships.

Later models are designed for use against both surface vessels and submarines. These have a great range and depth diving capacity, as well as a speed of 40 knots. Its guidance system is either acoustic homing, where it listens for its victim, then homes in on it, or wire-guided by a wire that remains attached to the parent submarine, through which it steers the torpedo to its target using its sonar.

Unlike the wire-guided torpedoes, the anti-ship missile Harpoon is a "fire and forget" weapon. It can be fired in salvos at several targets. Harpoon is designed to fit into an ordinary standard size torpedo tube. Upon firing, its outer shell breaks

Right: Standard wire-guided torpedo powered from the parent submarine through a single conducting wire with a return path passing back to the launching vessel through the sea

Below: A modern torpedo, showing the basic sections. This a shortened version, designed to allow more to be carried in a confined space.

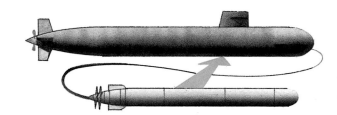

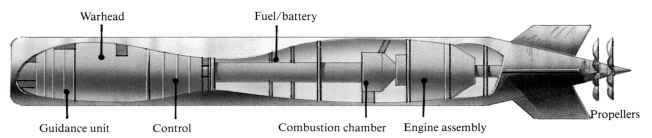

Warhead   Fuel/battery

Guidance unit   Control   Combustion chamber   Engine assembly   Propellers

Internal view of Harpoon

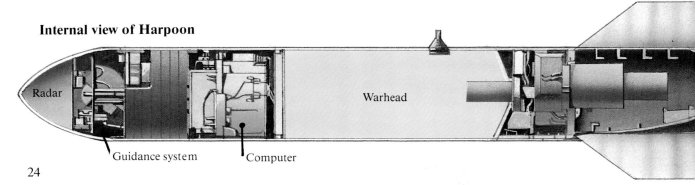

Radar

Warhead

Guidance system   Computer

away when it leaves the surface of the water. Harpoon then flies towards its target at wave-top level, well below enemy radar. Its casing, however, takes up valuable space within the torpedo tube and reduces the size of the missile itself.

A weapon especially developed for the use of US submarines is the anti-submarine missile Subroc. This is a nuclear stand-off weapon, fired through a torpedo tube. It has a range of 33.6 miles (56 km). After launching, it follows a short underwater course before breaking the surface and flying the main part of its journey to the target. At the appropriate moment, the depth charge separates from the rocket, dives back into the sea and sinks to a set depth before detonating.

Weapons such as these do not have to rely on a direct hit. They can be detonated some distance away from their target and thoroughly wreck it because of the effects of the nuclear fallout. A secondary effect of a nuclear explosion is to wipe out the control system on missiles and submarines not directly hit. This is enough to render them militarily useless.

Right: Six bow torpedo tubes of the Royal Navy's *Oberon* **class**

Below: Nuclear-armed SUBROC missile

Below: Harpoon shown in its case, with fins folded, ready for launching. It can be fired from a standard torpedo tube.

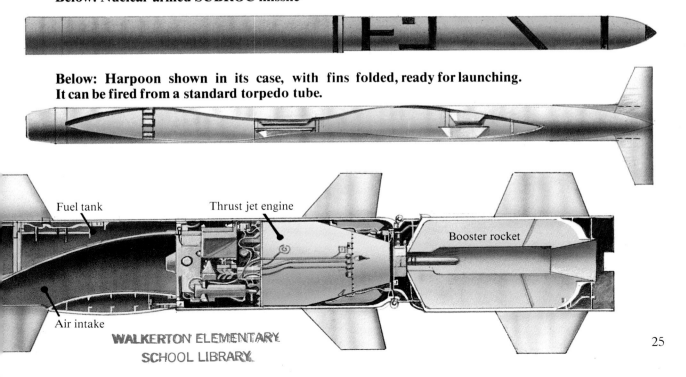

Fuel tank

Thrust jet engine

Booster rocket

Air intake

WALKERTON ELEMENTARY SCHOOL LIBRARY

11 Cruise Missiles

Cruise missiles are a further development of tactical weapons but have a greater range. Unlike ballistic missiles, cruise missiles do not leave the earth's atmosphere but fly on a low trajectory, or flight path, hugging the contours of the earth's surface.

Development of a submarine-launched cruise missile began in the 1950s. The US built the Regulus system which housed the missile, which looked like a small aircraft, in a large deck-mounted structure. This meant that the submarine had to be surfaced when it fired the missile and so exposed the submarine to attack. So this approach was abandoned.

By 1974 the US had begun to develop a more compact system called Tomahawk, which could be

Early Russian 'Whiskey' Long Bin with lengthened hull housing superimposed pairs of tubes

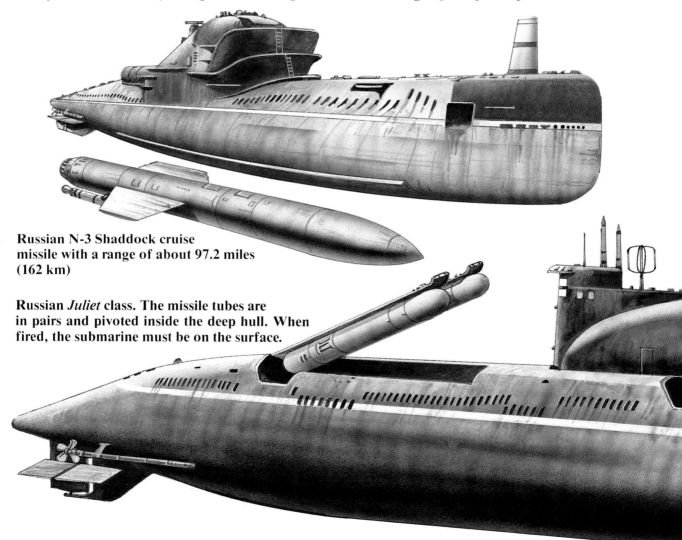

Russian N-3 Shaddock cruise missile with a range of about 97.2 miles (162 km)

Russian *Juliet* class. The missile tubes are in pairs and pivoted inside the deep hull. When fired, the submarine must be on the surface.

launched underwater and fitted a standard 21.32 inch (533 mm) torpedo tube. It came either with conventional explosive or a nuclear warhead for use against shipping or land targets. Tomahawk is driven by a turbofan engine and has a range of 420 to 1,500 miles (700 to 2,500 km) depending on the version. Its speed is 528 miles per hour (880 km per hour). In its anti-ship role it has a pre-programmed flight path to the target, followed by radar homing.

Originally Russian cruise missile submarines were produced in the 1950s to counter NATO carrier forces and the 1,400 ton *Whiskey Long Bin* class were the first in service. These early submarines had a modified fin which housed four SS-N-3 Shaddock tubes. The huge Shaddock missile is 42.9 feet (13 m) long, with a range of 120 miles (200 km) and carries a nuclear warhead.

The nuclear-powered *Echos* and diesel/electric *Juliet* submarines carry four SS-N-3 missiles in bins stowed flush with the deck and raised for firing. Deep indentations in the hull at the base of each bin act as blast deflectors. However, all these boats suffer from the disadvantage of having to surface to launch their missiles.

A second generation group, *Charlie* class, can fire their eight tubes submerged. Their SS-N-7s have a short range of only 27 miles (45 km) but are being superceded by SS-N-9s of double the range. These 29.172-foot (8.84-m), 44,990 pound (20,450 kg) solid fuel weapons are for use against surface ships. The 18,000 ton *Oscar* class are the latest development. They are armed with 24 missiles of the SS-N-19 type, with a range of 300 miles (500 km).

US Tomahawk surfacing

An early Russian *Echo* submarine with its launchers raised ready for firing

12
Strategic Missiles

Strategic missiles launched from submarines are probably the most technically advanced weapons system in existence. These submarine launched ballistic missiles (SLBMs) are designed for use against land targets. After firing, the missile leaves the earth's atmosphere for a time before returning and plunging onto a pre-determined target.

The early ballistic missiles, developed in the 1950s, were launched by solid fuel. This needed atmosphere in which to burn and so was unsuitable for use by submarines. In 1960, Polaris A1 was introduced, fired by cold gas which allowed the submarine to remain submerged and so hidden while launching missiles. With the introduction of this system, the face of deterrence was changed from a fixed land-based system that could be easily located, to a mobile system that could hide in the vast depths of the oceans.

There have been rapid strides in US missile development through Polaris 2 and 3, Poseidon of 1971, to today's Trident missile with a range of over 4,200 miles (7,000 km). Trident will be the US Navy's strategic missile of the next century.

From a late start, Russia has gained on the US to such an extent that their SS-N-18 missiles can threaten the US from anywhere in the world. France has developed her own missile program, while the United Kingdom uses US missiles but with UK warheads, though the size of French and UK forces bears no comparision with those of the superpowers.

UK 120+

France 80+

USA 760+

USSR 1154+

Number of missiles carried in total by the submarines of the four major navies of the world

Polaris   (US & UK)
Weight   34,927.2 pounds
          (15,876 kg)
Range   2,781 miles
          (4,635 km)

Poseidon (US)
Weight   64,867 pounds
          (29,485 kg)
Range   2,781 miles
          (4,635 km)

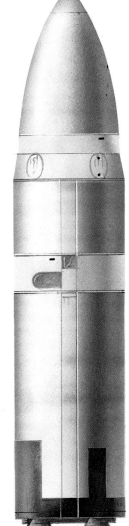

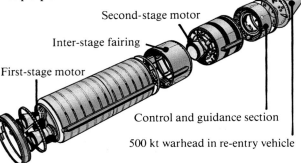

Second-stage motor

Inter-stage fairing

First-stage motor

Control and guidance section

500 kt warhead in re-entry vehicle

28

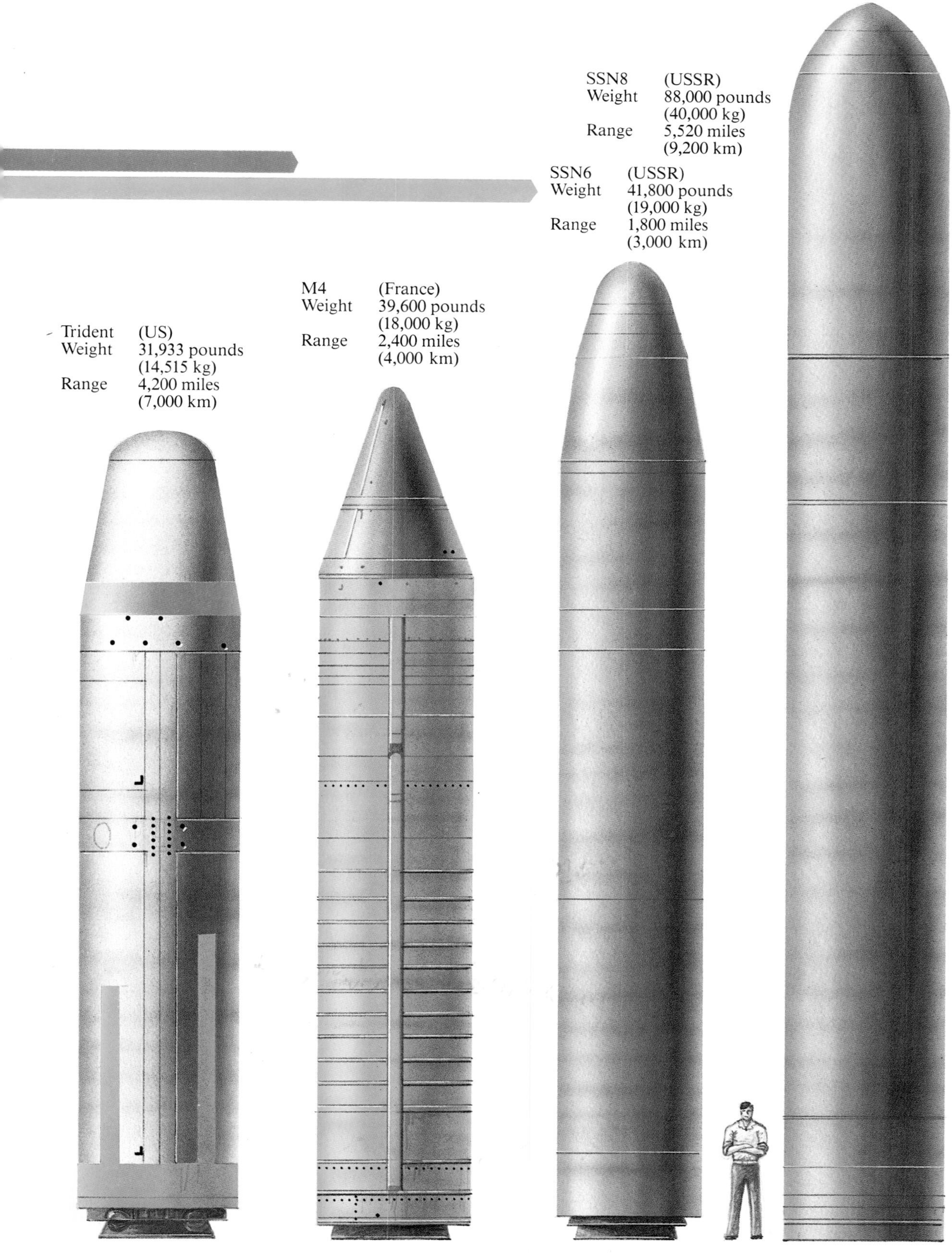

Trident (US)
Weight 31,933 pounds
(14,515 kg)
Range 4,200 miles
(7,000 km)

M4 (France)
Weight 39,600 pounds
(18,000 kg)
Range 2,400 miles
(4,000 km)

SSN8 (USSR)
Weight 88,000 pounds
(40,000 kg)
Range 5,520 miles
(9,200 km)

SSN6 (USSR)
Weight 41,800 pounds
(19,000 kg)
Range 1,800 miles
(3,000 km)

13 How the Missiles Are Fired

The missiles are housed upright snugly fitted into giant tubes set about midships in the submarine. Here the submarine's inertial guidance system (SINS) constantly keeps the information stored in the missile's own guidance system up to date.

Fire control computers work out the position of the ship in relation to targets and feeds this continuously into the missile's memory systems where the likely angle of attack (the trajectory) is constantly revised. In this way, the entire system is always ready for instant use.

When the hatch at the top of the missile tube is opened prior to firing, the tube is pressurized so that it does not flood. Cold gas forces the missile out of the tube and drives it until it leaps out of the

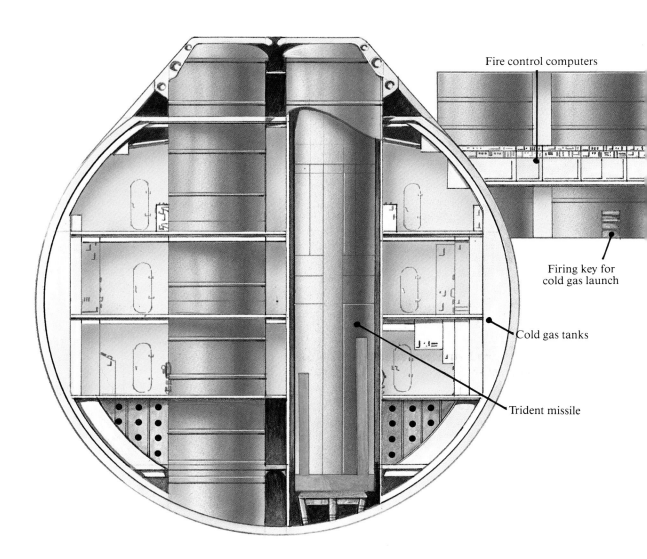

Fire control computers

Firing key for cold gas launch

Cold gas tanks

Trident missile

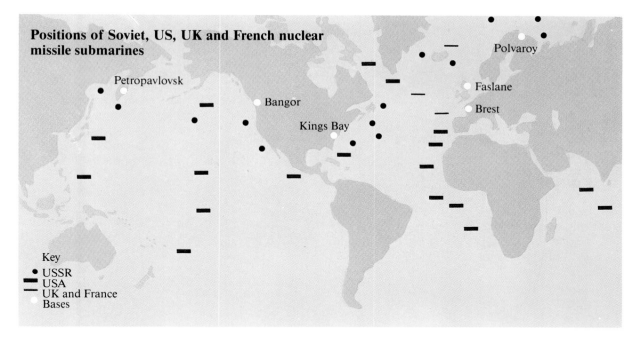

Positions of Soviet, US, UK and French nuclear missile submarines

Polvaroy

Petropavlovsk

Faslane

Bangor

Brest

Kings Bay

Key
- USSR
━ USA
━ UK and France
○ Bases

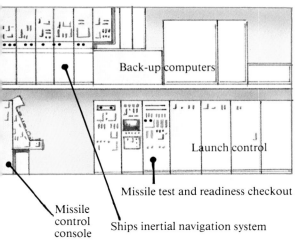

Back-up computers

Launch control

Missile test and readiness checkout

Missile control console

Ships inertial navigation system

Above: Launch and guidance control system for ballistic missiles

Left: Inside view showing how the US Trident missiles and their bins are housed. Note the large cold gas storage tanks running up the side of the hull. This gas is used to launch the missiles.

Nuclear missile submarine loading a Polaris missile at a shore base

sea. At this point, the missile's own rocket propulsion ignites and takes over and its navigation system guides it as it speeds towards its target many thousands of miles away, free from any outside control.

Missiles cannot be fired by accident. Only after the order to fire has been thoroughly checked and a complex sequence of commands from headquarters have been activated, will the captain of the missile submarine give permission for firing.

14 Hunting the Submarine

How an anti submarine group works
using all available systems for locating (yellow)
and attacking (red) a hostile submarine

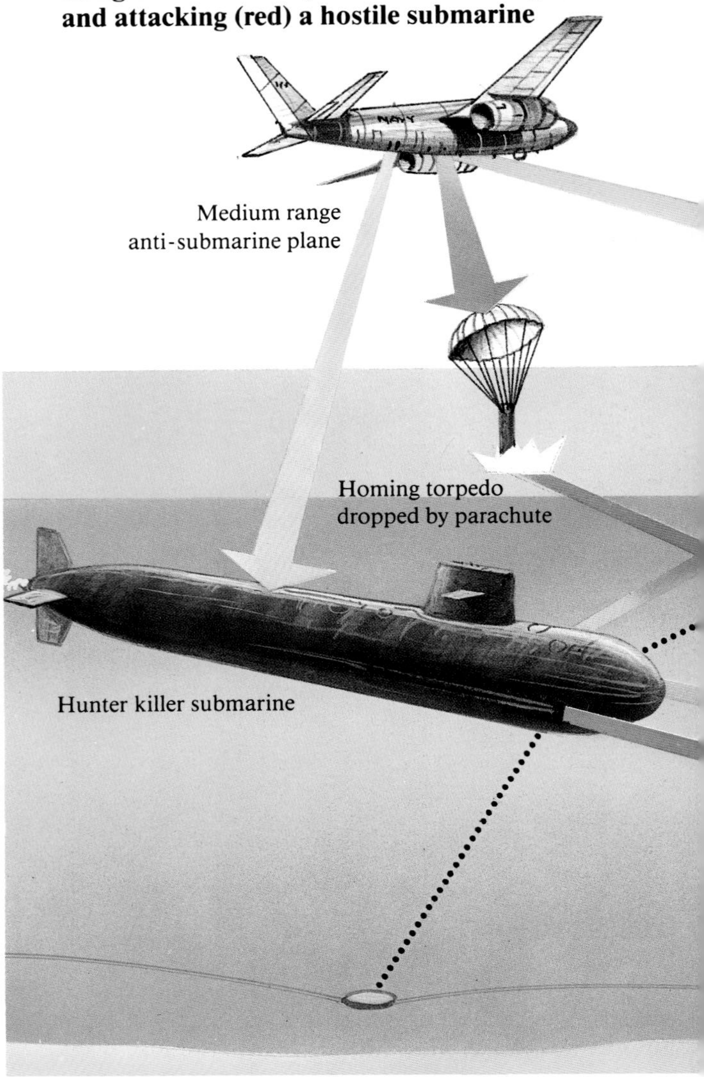

Medium range
anti-submarine plane

Homing torpedo
dropped by parachute

Hunter killer submarine

Missile submarines are considered a very real threat and great importance is placed on the task of locating and destroying them. This is one of the main jobs of a modern navy.

The first priority is to locate the enemy submarine and the main tool for doing this is sonar. Submarines moving in the ocean produce distinct noise effects, which can be detected by sophisticated listening systems. Hydrodynamic noise is created by the current of the water flowing over the submerged hull and rubbing against protrusions or free flood holes such as those seen in the top casing of Russian craft.

Nuclear submarines give off distinct machinery noise in spite of careful soundproofing. Propellers create noise and even the hull of the submarine can build up a magnetic field which can be picked up by sensitive detectors. In addition, disturbances of water as the submarine glides along can be picked up by satellite, by aircraft-mounted radar or by aircraft using special infrared equipment.

The complex systems used to track submarines are shown on the right. Chains of hydrophones rest on the seabed. These listening devices, linked to computers, are placed over wide areas of the ocean in an attempt to give an early warning of any submarine activity. Long-range sonar buoys, positioned along the edge of the continental shelf, scan the depths. Once the presence of a submarine has been indicated, destroyers will use their sonar equipment, helicopters will use their "dunking" sonars, and long range patrol aircraft will drop sonar buoys in an attempt to get a "fix."

The most effective search weapon is the submarine, which will scan the ocean with its passive or active sonar; while overhead, the orbiting satellite passes communications from one unit to another.

If a submarine thinks it is being hunted it will go silent, perhaps for days at a time. A modern submarine can go very quiet indeed, so that even a dropped tool would be a serious breach of silence.

Irregularities of the seabed and even shoals of fishes can help a submarine hide. In addition, water temperature can give the submarine protection. Cold water reflects back sonar waves, leaving an area where the submarine may hide. Warm water carries the sonar waves down so submarines have hull-mounted sensors to tell them the temperature of the water.

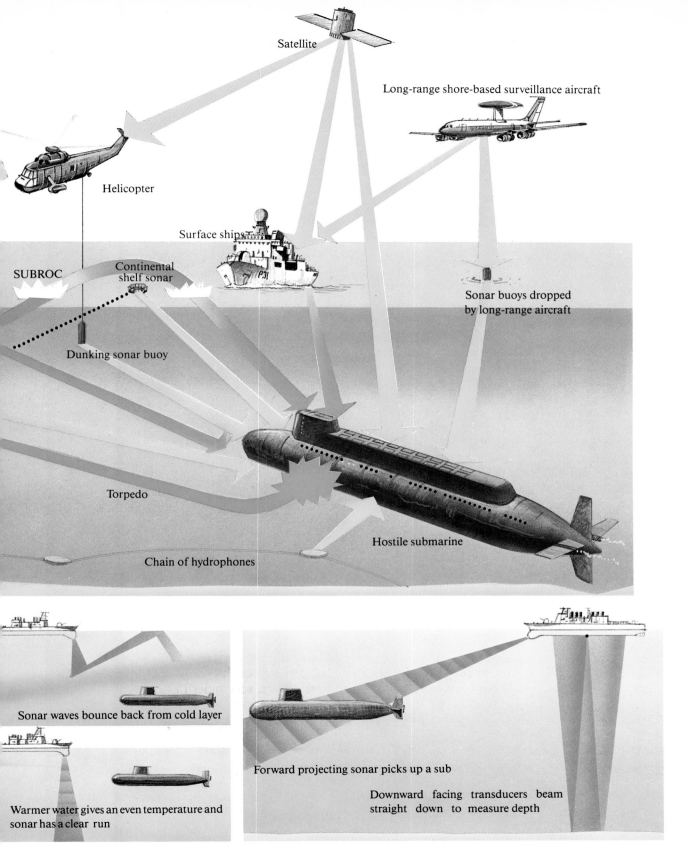

Satellite

Long-range shore-based surveillance aircraft

Helicopter

Surface ships

SUBROC

Continental shelf sonar

Sonar buoys dropped by long-range aircraft

Dunking sonar buoy

Torpedo

Hostile submarine

Chain of hydrophones

Sonar waves bounce back from cold layer

Warmer water gives an even temperature and sonar has a clear run

Forward projecting sonar picks up a sub

Downward facing transducers beam straight down to measure depth

15 Enemies of the Submarine

Carrier operated Grumman Hawkeye can oversee anti-submarine forces while detecting enemy air attacks.

Modern carriers devote much of their attention to anti-submarine warfare. They are the base for helicopters and tracker aircraft, which search for and attack the enemy submarines. Helicopters have proved to be one of the most efficient methods for tracking nuclear submarines. A typical US anti-submarine helicopter is the Sikorsky SH-60B Seahawk, carried by all major US warships. It is a versatile machine, using its dipping sonar to locate the enemy submarine, either by active "pinging" of ultrasonic echoes off the hull or by listening passively for propeller noise. Closely-spaced helicopters are an effective way of searching vast tracts of ocean and once found the helicopter, with three times the speed of the submarine, can keep pace with it. The helicopter can destroy the submarine with the two Mk 46 homing torpedoes that it carries.

A major Russian ASW helicopter is the Kamov KA 27 Helix, which is an improved version of the KA 25 Hormone. It carries uprated avionics, more weapons and sonobuoy capacity and has an increased radius of operation. This small compact helicopter can operate in any weather during day or night.

The US Navy now operates highly-specialized tracker aircraft from its carriers in the form of the S-3 Viking. These can carry an impressive range of detection equipment. Long waveband radars and infrared seekers can spot a submarine's snorkel, sonobuoys can be dropped to listen for propeller noise, and Magnetic Anomaly Detectors (MAD) can show how the submarine's hull is effecting the Earth's magnetism. The Viking carries a weapon load of four Mk 46 torpedoes and two Mk 57 depth charges.

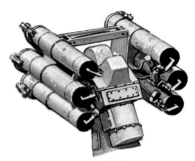

Above: Russian RBU-6000 twelve-barrel rocket launcher, range 6,000 m, carried on major surface ships

A land-based aircraft of great potential is the BAe(HSA) Nimrod with a twelve-hour endurance capacity, covering 5,556 miles (9,260 km) at 472.2 miles per hour (787 km/h) cruising speed. This type is being updated with Searchwater radar and new sonobuoy fit. It carries ASW torpedoes and depth bombs.

Anti-submarine surface vessels differ in size. The 10,000 ton Russian *Kara* class cruisers carry an imposing array of weapons and sensors. Gas turbines propel this vessel at 32 knots. Russian surface ships carry anti-submarine rockets which are fired in a pre-determined pattern by remote control from multi-rocket launchers.

Right: Typical anti-submarine frigate able to protect convoys and carrier groups. It provides a stable weapons platform in all weathers.

Top left: Compact Russian Kamov Ka 25 is only 34.32 feet (10.4m) long but carries a lethal array of anti-submarine weapons. Max speed 113 kts (209 km/h), endurance two hours.
Left below: Is Sikorsky SH-60 B Seahawk has an endurance of 3½ hours. Its speed is 140.4 miles per hour (234 km/h), weight 21,837.2 pounds (9,926 kg).

Complex sensor and weapon fit on a Russian *Kara Class* cruiser

Rocket launcher

SS-N-14 missile bins

Bow sonar

Variable depth sonar

1074

16 The Role of the Submarine in the Fleet

The nuclear-powered hunter/killer submarine forms an integral part of the modern task force, which usually has at its center a nuclear-powered aircraft carrier, surrounded by its attendant cruisers and destroyers in a protective screen, and with its full anti-submarine aircraft and helicopter cover operating overhead.

Within the fleet, the role of the submarine is to proceed ahead of the main force and to listen for any enemy submarines that may be trying to approach the fleet and break through the anti-submarine screen which protects it.

The key to success is quietness so that the hunter avoids detection while its own powerful sensors locate any opponents. All this may take place in an area well forward of the main fleet.

In the Navies of the world today there are over a thousand submarines of all types in service. The greatest number belong to Russia with 479 and the United States with 161.

Submarines of the World

Country	SS	SSG	SSB	SSN	SSGN	SSBN
Albania	3					
Argentina	9					
Australia	6					
Brazil	10					
Bulgaria	2					
Canada	3					
Chile	5					
China	113			6+		1+
Columbia	4					
Cuba	3					
Denmark	8					
Ecuador	2					
Egypt	20					
France	17		1	6		6
West Germany	24					
Greece	10					
India	16					
Indonesia	6					
Israel	6					

Country	SS	SSG	SSB	SSN	SSGN	SSBN
Italy	12					
Japan	18					
North Korea	19					
South Korea	5					
Libya	2					
Netherlands	8					
Norway	18					
Pakistan	11					
Peru	12					
Poland	4					
Portugal	3					
South Africa	3					
Spain	10					
Sweden	16					
Taiwan	2					
Turkey	10					
USSR	249	18	15	71+	63	79+
UK	16			17		9
USA	8			90	1	62
Venezuela	3					
Yugoslavia	6					

17
Captain and Crew Life Aboard the Submarine

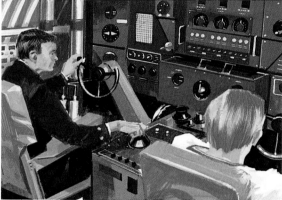

The demands of working in an entirely enclosed environment for lengthy periods coupled with the high degree of technical skill now required to work the sophisticated equipment in use mean that the crew members of submarines are a highly trained and expert team, ready to respond to any situation that arises.

The larger hulls of modern nuclear submarines can provide enough space for crew comfort to support the high endurance that the nuclear propulsion has made possible. The efficiency of the crew is related to the size of their accommodation. If it were possible to build smaller submarines, it would not follow that the crew kept in these confines would perform as well.

Missile submarines have two crews, one on duty, the other on leave. There are usually around 130 enlisted persons and twelve officers on board. Research into ventilation systems has shown that a submarine can remain continually submerged for three months, recycling its air. Paints are used that do not give off toxic fumes and colors are chosen with care to match harmoniously. As everything is

Above: Some aspects of life on a submarine. Crew have bunks with their own individual storage space amid crowded compartments. The control room has complex equipment showing how course, speed and depth are maintained.
Crew member standing by the relay control panel of a nuclear missile launching tube. Regular checks are carried out on this vital equipment and a high degree of skill is required by those who operate it.

viewed in artificial light, colors need to be bright. The only way of telling night from day on a submarine is that red lights are used at night.

The strain of long patrols is reduced by film facilities and gymnastic apparatus for exercise. But there is no communication with the outside world, no television or radio.

The strain placed upon a commanding officer of a nuclear missile submarine is very heavy. Only the captain and a few officers know where the submarine is to be stationed and in the hands of the captain rests the power to destroy millions of people should he receive the fatal order to loose the missiles. It is a difficult and exacting assignment and the commanding officer is highly trained for his role, though he may be a relatively young 35.

Serving as a commander of a nuclear-powered submarine is a demanding assignment requiring total concentration. Here, he manoeuvres his submarine alongside a tender ready to replenish supplies.

18 Submarine Rescue

Fortunately peacetime losses among submarine forces are rare, but in 1963 a US nuclear submarine the *Thresher* plunged about 1.2 miles (2 km) to the seabed after a steep diving maneuver had got out of control. Her crew of 129 men all died in the disaster as the submarine was reduced to a tangled mass of steel by the enormous pressure of seawater at that depth.

The US Navy had to find and salvage the vessel, but had no suitable rescue vehicles. They then set about designing a Deep Submergence Rescue Vessel (DSRV) which could be used in such an emergency.

The DSRV weighs about 32 tons, it is about 49.5 feet (15 m) long and can operate to 4,950 feet (1,500

4,200 ton submarine rescue ship *Ortolan*. It has an enormous beam to length ratio which provides a large deck working area over the twin catamaran hulls.

m) depth. The outer hull is made of formed fiberglass and contains three interconnected spheres that make up the main pressure capsule. These are made of high tensile steel. The forward sphere contains all the controls while the other two spheres can accommodate up to 24 survivors.

Transport aircraft usually airlift the DSRV to the nearest port to the disabled submarine. It is then taken by a surface support ship or submarine to the scene of the disaster. The DSRV descends to the injured submarine, using sonar, television and other advanced navigation aids. It positions its central sphere carefully in place over the rescue hatch, moving very accurately, using its side thrusters and rear propeller. Once in place, a collar is dropped over the rescue hatch and water is pumped out of it so that the submariners can transfer into the rescue vessel.

A submarine can carry and operate two of these craft, the DSRVs ferrying the rescued men back to the support submarine.

The US Navy has two *Pigeon* Class 4,200 ton surface vessels designed to assist in submarine rescue. They have twin catamaran hulls with a 34.32 feet (10.4 m) wide well in between and carry a heavy traveling crane amidships over the well for use in salvage operations. Ducted thrusters are installed in the bows to enable the vessel to maintain an accurate position when stationary. They can also operate the DSRV.

View of a striken submarine showing crew being rescued by a DSRV which has connected itself to the submarine's escape hatch. The parent rescue submarine hovers in the distance while a second DSRV also shuttles to and from the damaged craft.

19 Experimental and Naval Research Submarines

In the early 1960s a special projects office was set up in the US Navy to develop deep-ocean technology to support the missile-armed submarines of the Polaris and later Poseidon program. Developing a vehicle for research and recovery down to 4.2 miles (7 km) was one ambition of this project. It was never produced because of lack of resources; instead other deep submergence vehicles were acquired, notably the French *Trieste*.

The *Trieste* is the world's deepest diving submersible; it has descended to a depth of 6.547 miles (10.912 km). It was used in the Marianas Trench off Guam in the Pacific Ocean as part of a navy program of scientific and military study.

This craft has a forged steel observation pressure sphere attached to the base of a large float or container, rather like an airship, that holds gasoline. The gasoline, being lighter than water, lifts the craft to the surface after ballast in the form of nine tons of shot is released. The shot is stowed in two tubs within the float, held in position by electromagnets so that if the power fails the magnets no longer hold on and the craft floats to the surface.

In the 1960s deep submergence vehicles were used to recover a nuclear bomb from deep water off the coast of Spain after the aircraft carrying it crashed into the sea. This exercise took three months and cost millions of dollars to accomplish. In addition to the US Navy special purposes submarines, several commercial submarines were pressed into service, ranging from the US *Alvin* to the aluminum hulled *Aliminant* which was capable of diving to 2.743 miles (4.572 km). Specially-constructed deep sea platforms carrying powerful lights were able to penetrate the inky darkness of the sea at these depths and use their remote control arms to good effect. The entire exercise demonstrated the need for a special parent ship able to handle all the sophisticated equipment needed for the operation.

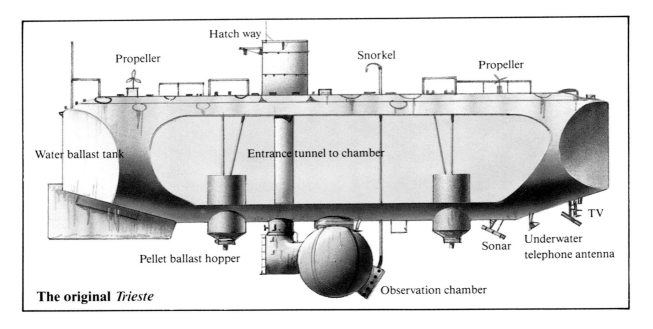

The original *Trieste*

US nuclear bombs being salvaged

Another experimental craft, shaped like the conventional submarine, is the 400 ton NR-1, used to test a small nuclear reactor. Special features include sonar for navigation and for the location of objects on the seabed. This vessel was used to recover an F14 fighter that accidentally rolled off the deck of an aircraft carrier and ended up nearly 2,145 feet (650 m) down on the seabed.

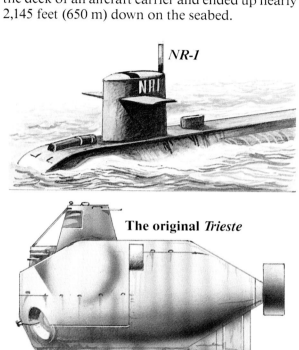

NR-1

The original *Trieste*

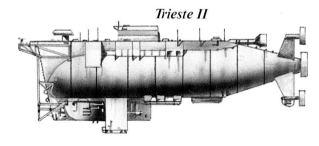

Trieste II

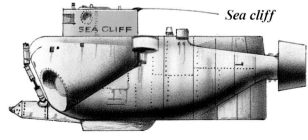

Sea cliff

20
Support Ships

In addition to operating out of a land based establishment with all the facilities available, a submarine may have to rely on the service and backup of a surface vessel.

The US Navy has twelve submarine support ships which are used with different types of submarines. The 22,000 ton *L Y Spear* class has five units especially designed to handle the *Los Angeles* class of attack submarines. They can service four of them, moored alongside at the same time. They have a helicopter platform and carry satellite receivers, along with missiles for self defense. Enough stores are carried to supply twelve submarines

Older tenders are being modernized, such as the 21,000 ton *Simon Lake* which can handle three nuclear missile submarines simultaneously, including the stowage of nuclear missiles.

The *Huntley* class also handle SSBNs making full use of the 52 workshops available. Although slightly smaller at 19,000 tons, each of these vessels originally cost $25 million.

Russia possesses a number of smaller submarine tenders from the 9,500 ton *Volga* class to the 20-year-old *Dnepr* class. These vessels can carry out repairs and although they have quarters for 450 submariners, they are not as sophisticated as their US counterparts.

One of the large US submarine tenders able to handle several ballistic missile submarines at a time

21 The Future

The major development of the nuclear-powered submarine will be the increased quietness of the craft; this is made vital by the sophistication of the listening devices becoming available. Russia will continue her quest for higher underwater speeds and greater operating depths. The newly-built titanium-hulled submarines are a step in this direction. Work on power plants continually progresses and the compact Russian unit is based on a liquid metal nuclear reactor.

Conventional propellers greatly add to noise above 12 knots, so future submarines could have pump jets for high speed passive operation.

Conventional submarines will probably hover around the 2,500 to 3,000 ton mark, with greater automation in order to reduce the number of crew.

Certain designs will lend themselves to specialization so that some boats will only carry torpedoes while sister vessels will have a missile belt, enabling them to carry cruise missiles of an even more potent type. This will mean that smaller, relatively cheaper boats can be built, each with special roles but incorporating all the latest technology.

In the quest for greater speed, changes in the tail configuration to the X shape are likely, as well as the use of special anechoic coating. New US submarines are likely to be beamier in width and shorter in length, with the proportions of the earlier fast *Skipjack* design.

Finally, should Third World powers ever acquire nuclear weapons, the submarine might well be seen as the ideal system for delivery.

Glossary

ASW
Anti Submarine Warfare, a term covering all aspects of the detection and destruction of enemy submarines

BATTERIES
An arrangement of cells which supply electric current while the submarine is submerged. They are recharged when the submarine uses its main surface propulsion.

CLASS
A group of vessels built to the same design

CONTINENTAL SHELF
A sort of raised platform standing higher than the seabed and covered by shallow seas with depths of up to 660 feet (200 m) off the seaboard of a continent

CRUISE MISSILE
A short to medium range missile powered by some form of jet engine that is winged and guided throughout its flight. It is able to fly very low, avoiding detection by enemy radar. It can carry nuclear warheads, mainly for use against land targets, or fitted with explosives for use against surface ships.

DEPTH CHARGE
A form of bomb or canister containing explosives used to attack submarines that when dropped from an aircraft or surface vessel will fall to a preset depth before exploding. Some are fitted with nuclear warheads, some have sensors which trigger the depth charge when it is near a submarine.

DIESEL ENGINE
Internal combustion engine that uses crude oil. It has a low flash point which makes it safe to use in the confined space of a submarine. The engine works by burning diesel to generate steam which then powers turbines. The turbines drive an electric motor which drives the propellers.

DSRV
Deep Submergence Rescue Vessel. A specially-designed small submarine able to descend to great depths and lock onto the rescue hatch in a stricken submarine, so allowing trapped crew to escape.

DUCTED THRUSTERS
Small motors or propellers able by means of angling to make subtle changes in the main direction in which the craft is traveling

FIN
Narrow superstructure on the submarine, housing the main sensing equipment such as periscopes, radar, etc. It also has a shallow cockpit for use by the commanding officer while the submarine is surfaced.

HARPOON
A sea-skimming missile that can be fired from a torpedo tube. It has an outer case that breaks open when the missile leaves the water. A solid fuel rocket then takes over and the missile flies to its target by radar guidance.

HYDROPHONES
Microphones that pick up underwater sounds and convert them into electrical impulses for transmission

HYDROPLANES
Small wing-like fins which are used for controlling a submarine's angle and depth

INFRARED
A sensitive optical device that is able to provide a clear image in a periscope in bad visibility or at night

MAD
Magnetic Anomoly Detection system, used to detect submerged submarines. A MAD receiver is carried over the sea, for example on a long pole behind an aircraft, and is designed to detect the very small change in the Earth's local magnetism caused by the large metal hull of a submarine.

MINE
An underwater explosive that is usually anchored to the seabed at a certain depth in areas of known submarine activity. It explodes when struck by a vessel, or if fitted with a proximity sensing device, when a ship is nearby. Some mines are fitted with nuclear warheads.

NUCLEAR POWER
A very high energy fuel that needs no oxygen for its combustion and so gives a submarine the ability to remain submerged almost indefinitely

PERISCOPE
An optical instrument that enables the viewer to see objects that are not in his line of vision. By a series of mirrors and prisms that reflect the light, the periscope reveals what is on the surface of the sea while the submarine is submerged.

POLARIS
A two-stage intermediate-range nuclear-armed ballistic missile fired from a submerged submarine. First installed by the US in 1956.

POSEIDON
The successor to Polaris, the second generation nuclear-armed intercontinental ballistic missile developed by the US for use by submarines

RADAR
RAdio Detection And Ranging, a method for detecting the position and speed of a distant object. A narrow beam of very high frequency radio pulses is transmitted and reflected by the object back to the transmitter. The direction of the beam and the time between transmitting and receiving the pulse back, give the position of the object.

RANGE
The distance a submarine can travel for a given speed and fuel supply

REACTOR
The specially sealed structure which houses and generates the nuclear power. Special precautions ensure that no leaks occur.

RUDDER
Upright fin at the stern of the submarine which enables the boat to be steered

SAIL
US term for conning tower, the superstructure of a submarine

SATELLITE
An earth-orbiting piece of equipment stationed in the upper atmosphere of the earth that can receive and relay messages or locate objects far below on the earth's surface

SHADDOCK
A Soviet cruise missile carried on submarines and cruisers

SINS
Ships Internal Navigation System

SNORKEL
A breathing tube through which submarines can take in or expel air. A valve in the tube prevents water from entering the submarine.

SONAR
SOund NAvigation RAnging, or echo sounding. An instrument that sends out regular sound signals, which bounce back from solid objects giving a signal that registers on a screen.

SONAR BUOY
A buoy equipped with a sonar system designed to detect enemy submarines by listening for any sounds that reflect back from them. Each distinctive submarine or ship has its own sonar signature that is programmed into the system. Helicopters use dunking sonarbuoys when searching for submarines. These send signals back to the helicopters.

SS
A conventional submarine propelled by a diesel-electric engine

SSB
A conventionally-powered ballistic missile submarine

SSBN
A nuclear-powered ballistic missile submarine

SSG
A conventionally-powered cruise missile submarine

SSGN
A nuclear-powered cruise missile submarine

SSN
A nuclear-powered attack submarine

STRATEGIC WEAPONS
Long-range nuclear weapons aimed at civilian and military targets

SUBROC
A US submarine-launched nuclear missile which leaves the water, travels at supersonic speed through the air, then dives back into the water to attack

TACTICAL WEAPONS
Those for use in battle against another submarine or ship

TEARDROP HULL
The design of modern submarine hulls, with a full rounded bow, tapering away towards the stern

TENDER
A parent ship able to replenish a submarine's supplies and provide accommodation for crew. It is also able to carry out repairs.

TITANIUM
An extremely strong yet lightweight metal able to withstand the great pressures exerted on a hull deep in the ocean

TOMAHAWK
A US cruise missile that can be launched from submarines from a standard torpedo tube

TORPEDO
A self-propelled weapon that is fired from a tube in a submarine by compressed air. It follows an underwater path to its target.

TRAJECTORY
The angle of flight of a missile from its launch to its target. It may be flat, following the surface of the sea of the contours of the land, or a high trajectory.

TRIDENT
One of the most recent submarine-launched ballistic missiles developed by the US

TRIM TANKS
Small tanks set within a submarine that maintain the submarine at a precise depth by being filled or emptied of sea water

TURBOJET/TURBOFAN
The turbojet engine is a jet engine in which a turbine-driven compressor draws air into the engine which compresses it into a combustion chamber, fuel being injected at the same time. The hot gases produced rush to the rear and drive the turbine before leaving at high velocity through the rear. A more recent development is the turbofan in which some of the incoming air is bypassed round the combustion chamber and accelerated rearwards by a turbine-operated fan to mix with exhaust gases from the combustion chamber, so increasing thrust without increasing fuel consumption.

TURRET
A small lightly-armored structure on a submarine for housing artillery

Index

WALKERTON ELEMENTARY
SCHOOL LIBRARY